MILDRED'S MINDSET

Wisdom from a Woman Centenarian

Mildred Kirschenbaum

with Gayle Kirschenbaum

Kirschenbaum Productions, LLC
New York, NY

Sketch of Mildred by her daughter Gayle
Circa 1970s

CONTENTS

APPRECIATION

This book would have never been realized if it hadn't been for Mildred's fans. Comments like these are what inspired me to sit down with my mother and put pen to paper:

> "You mother's wisdom is priceless. I don't personally know anyone who has reached the century mark, much less a person who has reached their 100th birthday and is a rock star on social media. She is a gift to all of us, a true leader on this planet."

> "Mildred, you are such an inspiration: not only for other seniors, but for us upcoming seniors! Keep on living life to the fullest! Never stop sharing your stories!!"

> "Wise, wise woman! Thank you!"

> "Words to live by!"

> "You are a role model! God bless you!"

Every effort was made to produce this book in a timely matter, given the age of its author. Mom was already 100 years old and I wanted her to enjoy the glory of holding her book - showcasing her wisdom - in her hand. And to still be able to go on a book tour, meet her fans, and sign their books.

It takes a team to put out a beautiful book.

Acclaimed origami artist Marc Kirschenbaum brilliantly designed the book, including the front cover and interior, and meticulously formatted it and created all the illustrations. Moreover, he fastidiously cleaned up each of the over 64 photos, which span a hundred years. Considering the age of some of the images, one can only imagine their initial condition. I'm eternally grateful to him for the artistry and elegance he infused into shaping the appearance of this book. Cover designer David Ter-Avanesyan skillfully helped us shape the back cover.

Copy editor Tina Buckman saved me from embarrassment by placing commas in the right places, teaching me about using em dashes, and helping me rephrase sentences to make them clearer. This task was further assisted by editor Melanie Gall, making sure we didn't miss anything.

Additionally, Tina Buckman, who is also a photographer, used her keen eye to help me curate the photos.

Publisher Naomi Rosenblatt of Heliotrope Books generously shared advice on marketing, as did publicist Jennifer A. Maguire. Along the way, I picked the brain of authors who gave me invaluable tips. I can't thank them enough.

I want to thank Mom's fans for encouraging us to move quickly and for supporting this effort. Without them, this book would never have been realized.

As a testament to the collaborative spirit and dedication of everyone involved, this book embodies the indispensable roles each person played, and we are profoundly grateful.

PROLOGUE

Each time my mother came out with one of her one-liners, I rushed to write it down. Many times, though, I wasn't quick enough.

"They come out of me fast. And then I forget them," my mother explained.

I'm grateful for what I remembered and/or recorded, making it possible for me to share them with you.

My mother is a phenomenon in many ways. Or, as my brother says, "She's an anomaly." It's rare to meet a woman who is so with-it at 100 years of age. Even her body is that of a much younger woman—never mind her brain.

The 2006 death of my father, to whom she was married for 64 years, marked the turning point in our relationship. My mother was alone for the first time in her life and I knew in my heart that I would be there for her. I told my father, on his deathbed, not to worry. I would take care of Mom.

But I knew that in order to show up for her, I would have to learn how to handle her snarky remarks and criticisms. Especially those targeted at me. I did this by figuring out the secret to finding forgiveness. It allowed me to take off my victim hat and reframe how I saw my mother, which led me to feel compassion towards her. By changing how I reacted to insults, our relationship was transformed.

Over the past several years we have traveled the world together, including adventurous trips to India, the Middle East, Europe, and South America.

We made a film together called *Look At Us Now, Mother!* which follows my journey of forgiveness. She became known to some as "that despisable mother," and to others, she was seen as brave for putting herself out there. She walked down many red carpets, received dozens of roses, and was photographed and interviewed all over the world.

After a standing ovation at the sneak première, which was the first time she saw the film, my mother came to the stage and looked out at the audience. Then she said, "I never knew I was such a bitchy mother."

When asked at the cocktail party what her next picture was, she said, "Porn."

I launched my Instagram account to showcase my fine art photography. It was growing . . . slowly. When my mother turned 99 years old, I aimed my phone at her and asked her how it felt to be that age. I posted her response, and to my amazement, it went viral. I then decided to dedicate my Instagram to my mother and to launch a TikTok account focused on her, her wisdom, and our relationship.

Since Covid, I have been dividing my time between my home in New York and my mother's home in Florida. She is quite savvy with many things, including technology. I gave her a quick lesson on how to videotape herself on her phone, and now she sends her recordings to me, I edit them to length, and post them.

One video shocked me. Looking directly at the camera, my mother said, "Gayle, you are so talented. You are an extraordinary filmmaker and a wonderful artist. You know how proud I am of you. You will never know. But yes, I was very harsh in so many ways and for that, I ask your forgiveness. In my heart, I know you forgave me but now I am trying to forgive myself. I loved you from the day you were born and will love you until the day I die and then I will watch you from afar."

My mother had finally confessed her wrongdoings. Fans were in awe of her words, saying they wished they had heard this sort of confession and apology from their denigrating mothers. In many cases it was too late; their mothers were already long deceased.

Mom and I became a formidable team of social media influencers. She is the longevity expert, and I'm the forgiveness coach. Together, we are the poster mother/daughter for a happy, positive, and mutually rewarding relationship.

As Mom often says in our videos, "We are not only mother and daughter, we are best friends."

I'm in awe that I can co-create this book with my mother and my best friend: centenarian sensation, Mildred Kirschenbaum.

Our mission is to bring joy, laughter, and wisdom into your life.

Gayle

MEET MILDRED

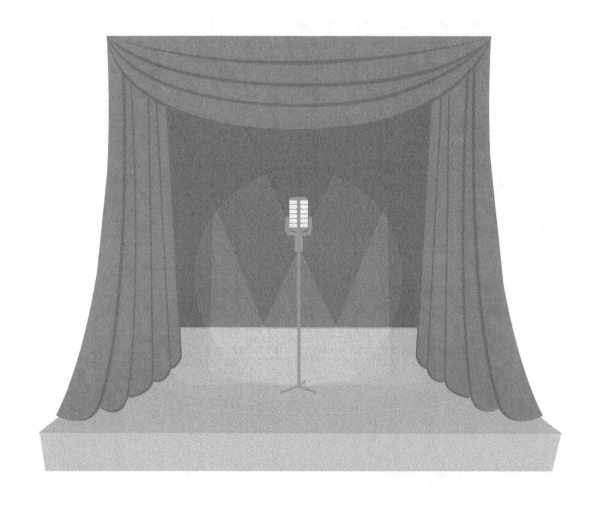

Mildred Kirschenbaum was born in August 1923 in Brooklyn, New York, to immigrants from Poland and Lithuania. She came out of the womb with a zest for life, into a loving family that faced several hardships.

Mildred said, referring to the death of her infant sister, "She caught pneumonia from a neighbor's child. If that had happened today, they would have given her penicillin, and she would have lived."

When twelve-year-old Mindala, also known as Mildred, rushed home from a party, she nearly tripped over a man being carried out on a stretcher. It turned out to be her father, who had attempted suicide. It was his second try. Mildred explained, "This was after the Depression and my father's business was suffering. He was concerned about providing for his family and thought the money from his life insurance would provide for them, not realizing there was a clause for suicide."

With Mildred's father now bedridden with depression, her mother didn't wallow in pity. Instead, she took action. She opened up a produce store and worked to feed her family.

Mildred went to an academic high school called Girls High. She took up the violin and after graduation got a job in the garment center. "I felt my mother worked all the years supporting me and I had to at least support myself. I did a little modeling. And then some sales. My mother insisted I go to Brown's Business College and take up stenotype for court reporting. I hated typing and transcribing my notes. That reminds me, I lent my stenotype machine to someone years ago and never got it back."

A svelte, stylish, and smart 17-year-old, Mildred was introduced to Gerry Kirschenbaum. Everyone had heard of the Kirschenbaums, as they owned a well-known funeral home in Brooklyn. Red-headed Gerry was a head-turner, with his light blue eyes and athletic body. Within a year, World War II broke out. The lovebirds eloped before Gerry was shipped to the South Pacific to fight. "During my time, if you wanted to have sex, you got married," Mildred justified her teenage marriage.

Four years later, upon Gerry's safe return, Mildred ended up pregnant with the first of their three children. Being a young mother during the 1940s, 50s, and 60s, Mildred took on many roles. Not only did she do the cooking, but she brilliantly managed their finances, she did most of the handiwork (including fixing appliances and making the curtains and bedspreads), and she even built a bar for the den.

One day, when Mother was already in her 80s, I called her. She answered the phone and said, "Oh, Gayle, I was out in the garden fixing the light. I just told your father he won't know whether to replace me with a man or a woman."

Gerry was not a big earner, but Mildred knew how to stretch a dollar. "Each week when your father got paid and it was cash, he took what he wanted and gave me the rest. I would tuck a little money away each week in different savings accounts. I had one for vacations and one for the Bar Mitzvahs. When the gifts came in from the Bar Mitzvahs, I put that money into a separate savings account for education. From those savings, we paid for all your brothers' colleges, law school, podiatry school, and your college, including books and housing."

16

Ever since Mildred was young, she had always been stylish. Even without much money, she managed to look like a million bucks. "I learned from my mother. She didn't have a pot to piss in, but she always put herself together nicely. I remember when I was a little girl and my father was sick and we needed help. She asked her brother for a loan and he said, 'You don't look poor.'"

A savvy shopper, Mother frequented Loehmann's, a discount clothing store that first opened in Brooklyn in 1921. Mrs. Frieda Loehmann made deals with high-end manufacturers to sell their merchandise at much lower prices, with the designer labels cut out. Loehmann's was a feeding frenzy for women. As they didn't have dressing rooms then, the aisles were packed with women trying on clothing. Mom was there so often that I was convinced I was born there.

Mildred's creativity went beyond her fashionista skills. By the time she got done furnishing our home, it could have been featured in Architectural Digest. Great at scavenging in antique stores, Mom insisted on traveling to upstate New York to search for her treasures.

If she saw something she loved and the price was right, no matter how large it was, no matter how much work it needed, she bought it. This is when Dad would belt out, "How the hell are you going to get that home?"

"We will, don't worry," Mom would respond as she paid for the eight-foot French Baroque gilded wood-framed mirror. And she did always manage to get it home—often tying the item on top of their 1960s Catalina Pontiac. Mildred was also highly skilled at packing, wrapping, and roping. She could tie any kind of knot and would firmly secure her treasures to the car roof.

Dad would scream the whole ride home, stretching his arm out the window to make sure the rope was secure. This probably contributed to his high blood pressure.

Mildred's natural leadership skills were unleashed when she started working with nonprofits. She became president of the Sisterhood at her Temple and vice-president of the Cerebral Palsy chapter in her county. Mildred often found herself standing at the podium giving speeches. "I always needed a good opening line that I dug up from something I read. After that, I didn't need notes and could just go on and on."

Often when I asked Mom a question and she didn't respond immediately, she said, "I'm thinking. Don't you smell the wood burning?"

Mildred had a thirst for travel, and in the 1970s she and a couple of partners decided to open up a travel agency. This was before the Internet. As travel agents they got many deals, and she would go off with Dad and sometimes with me. Their adventures included a safari in West Africa, a trip behind the Iron Curtain, and cruises all over the world.

Nothing stopped Mildred, and she didn't care what people thought of her. One day when she was working at the travel agency, a client called to complain about her. Mildred grabbed the phone and said to the disgruntled customer, "The only person I report to is God."

When it was time for retirement, Mildred and Gerry left New York and settled in southern Florida. "I have everything at my fingertips here. I'm in an adult sleepaway camp," Mildred raved about her country club living.

Mildred, who is all about looking good, instructed her plastic surgeon before her facelift: "I don't want my money's worth. You don't have to pull, pull, and pull." Then, years later, she returned to the doctor and said, "Look at my face. It's like a roadmap. What do we do now?" She was already close to 90 at this time and decided not to pursue anything else. Although in her 90s, she did redo her tattooed eyeliner that was fading and had her eyebrows tattooed on.

Dad passed away in 2006, leaving 83-year-old Mildred with a lot of life to live. At the time of his death, they had been together for 64 years. It wasn't unusual for people to ask her, "What was the secret to your long marriage?" Without missing a beat, she always responded, "Never go to sleep angry."

Once, when I was visiting my mother, I questioned her friends about my dad. At the time, Mother and her posse were enjoying Happy Hour at their clubhouse. One girlfriend told me, "I loved your father. He was a very handsome man and dressed impeccably."

Mildred, already inebriated, announced in a voice so loud that the next room could hear her, "I used to go to sleep every night of my marriage holding his schmuck (penis)." Perhaps *that* was her secret to their long marriage.

One day while at the checkout at the grocery store, Mother was searching in her purse. When I asked what she was looking for, she responded, "A picture of a dead president." She pulled out a twenty-dollar bill.

When Mom and I were both single, we decided to turn to Craigslist to see if, working as a team, we could find love again. As I started writing the ad, I read it out loud: "Hip Senior Mother and Hip Middle-Aged Daughter Seek Father and Son." Mother added, ". . . Who Are Breathing."

When we called a man who responded to our ad, we learned he was the father, 48 years old, and his son was 25. Mom responded to him about his son, "He's so young I could chew him up and spit him out."

At Mom's 90th birthday party, she climbed onto the bar waving her pink boa.

After the death of my father, Mom and I began traveling the world together. Our escapades took us to many places, including India, the Middle East, South America, and Europe. Mother often shares with others, "Gayle is not only my best friend but my favorite travel companion. There isn't anyone else I would like to travel with."

We are two strong women (note: the apple doesn't fall far from the tree - like mother, like daughter). We can go at it like two feisty cats, hissing and scratching. And then, five minutes later, curl up together like nothing happened. According to Mom, "We're like an old married couple. Despite all our arguments, we never stop talking."

Mildred doesn't suffer fools well. At nearly 100 years old, Mother was in her bank waiting a long time for help. It left her infuriated with the incompetency of the teller. She told me later, "If I killed her, I'd get life, and they would be cheated."

When Mom and I aren't together, we speak numerous times a day. One day, when Mom was 99, she called to tell me, "I made an executive decision. When I die, bury me with my phone so you can call me."

At 100, Mildred is still living alone in her home. She has an active life. She drives, plays cards and mahjong, does her marketing, manages her financial portfolio, and never misses a Happy Hour.

One day her washing machine broke. Mom, nearly 100 years old at the time, pulled the soaking wet sheets and towels out of the machine and threw them into bags. She carried this heavy load into a laundromat. I was about to order a new machine for her online, and she alerted me, "No, Gayle, I want to go to the store and see it first. I'll go to Home Depot." It was already 3:30 p.m. when she finished her laundry and realized it was Monday night – meatball night.

Mom headed right over to Lynora's and found herself a seat at the crowded bar. She ordered her vodka and tonic and their Monday night Happy Hour food special, $3.00 meatballs. Then she turned to the young man in his fifties sitting next to her and said, "I'm ninety-nine and a half. I'm not picking you up, but would you like to talk?" They gabbed for a long time before he had to go home to his wife. When Mom asked for her check, she was advised that the gentleman next to her had paid. "Oh!

Can you tell me how much it was so I can leave you a gratuity?"
she asked. "He took good care of us," the bartender said.

This wasn't the first time Mother had her order paid for by
a complete stranger she just met and apparently charmed.
There isn't a topic Mildred can't speak on, as she keeps herself
informed about nearly everything. She often lifts her glass at a
friendly Happy Hour bar. "Here's to those who wish me well,
and those who don't can go to Hell!" As she makes her toast,
her fellow customers all break out in laughter.

One day, when I was visiting Mom, I got into bed with her on
what had been my father's side. I felt some hard objects under
me and pulled out an iPad, three TV remote controls, and an
iPhone. Mother spends hours on her devices playing bridge, as
well as word and number games. "It keeps my mind sharp," she
explained as I encouraged her not to play in the middle of the
night because it keeps her up and alert for hours.

"You know, if I took away your iPad you'd have a temper
tantrum," I told Mom.

"I have an announcement to make. I think we're getting a
divorce," Mother informed me.

On one morning call, Mom told me, "I took a shower and a
shit. I'm nice and clean inside and out."

In the midst of another conversation, I was excited to share a
recent family genealogy discovery I had made. "The only roots I
care about are my hair roots," Mom let me know. Then she said,
"I have to go pee. The rain outside is an inspiration."

Tech-savvy Mildred, whose several devices include a Windows laptop, complained one day, "My computer is so slow that the grass isn't growing."

As a thriving centenarian, she was asked about her exercise routine by a fan. "I exercise my mouth daily," she responded.

On a more poignant note, when talking about someone, she said, "If they are worth my anger, they are worth my love."

PHOTOS

31

33

MINDSET

MILDRED'S MINDSET

100 Years of Living and Wisdom

As Mom and I have become close, I have taken to recording our life, our story, and tips from my mother. Then I post them on social media. Mildred's fans are eager to know what her secrets are to longevity and they relish in her wisdom.

ATTITUDE

Look at the positive side of life. I think that is what got me so far. I try my best not to sweat the small stuff and to have a positive attitude. I have friends who are twenty or thirty years younger than me and their attitude is going to cause them not to survive to my age. They are not grateful for anything. They complain they don't see their kids more than once a week, the meal served is cold, or it is bad. Their attitude is not acceptable. If the food is not quite right, then have an extra dessert. If you only hear from your kids once a week, that's fine. They call you once a week and you call them once a week. Be grateful they are enjoying life.

Change your attitude and look at the positive side of life.

Don't be a Monday morning quarterback. What's done is done. Sometimes it's difficult to have a good attitude when someone is not being nice to you. I try my best to ignore them.

LEARN NEW THINGS

No matter your age, don't be afraid of learning new things. You have to move with the times. Learn how to use a computer, a smartphone, and a notebook. I use a PC, an iPhone, and an iPad. With these devices, I am able to do online banking, trade stocks, and manage my portfolio. Plus, they allow me to keep up to date on the news. I play bridge, Words with Friends, Numfeud, and Wordle on my devices. I read books and periodicals.

My mind is always working. When I have a problem with any of my technology, I contact support and it gets resolved. I use YouTube videos to learn how to fix things that break in my house. If I need to change the battery on a Ring bell, I read the directions or watch a YouTube video. I have several smart TVs and I know my way around them.

Keep your mind going.

COMMUNITY

I'm fortunate that I live in a gated community with a clubhouse where I play bridge, canasta, pan, and mahjong. That keeps me busy and my mind active, and it's very social. By joining these games, I've gained a circle of friends. We go out to dinner together, but we also check on one another. If someone misses the game, we quickly investigate to see what's happened.

No matter where you live, even if you are alone in an apartment building without services, there are always opportunities to meet people and avoid solitude. You can meet others at community centers and houses of worship, which exist in most places. Since the pandemic, many have turned to joining groups online, some of which are hybrid, also offering in-person attendance if you prefer. The crucial thing is to build relationships with others and foster friendships to avoid isolation. Studies have shown that having community is one of the keys to longevity.

SIDESTEP RESTRICTIONS

During the pandemic, when our club was closed and we were all in lockdown, I started a 5:00 p.m. cocktail hour on my driveway. I bought individual packages of snacks. Everyone arrived with their own glass and chair. We each sat six feet apart and enjoyed a drink, a snack, and most importantly, conversation and connection with other humans. People told me that they couldn't wait for 5:00 p.m. to come each day.

KNOW YOUR LIMITATIONS

At 100 years old, I still drive and am fortunate to have good reflexes. I no longer drive long distances and avoid night driving, except within my gated community. I am very alert when behind the wheel. I use all my mirrors, signal at turns, and am aware of what those around me are doing. I know my driving skills are good because once a week, my neighbors, who are my children's age, ask me to pick them up to go the clubhouse where we play cards.

When I go shopping for groceries, I make sure to have only a few items packed in each bag so they are easy for me to carry. Even though I end up with more bags, they're light enough for me to lift.

As I've aged, I've lost strength in my hands, making it challenging to open jars and containers that were never an issue before. I use a couple of different types of grippers. If that doesn't work and it's not an immediate necessity, I leave the jar out. When I see one of the gardeners or sanitation workers, I ask them to help, and they are more than happy to assist.

HAPPY HOUR

I go to Happy Hour because it is very social. There are times I go alone. I sit near people; preferably I try to get a seat in the middle of the bar, so I can talk to people. Not only do I get my drinks and often food at a discount, but I make new acquaintances and have interesting conversations. I stay away from talking politics because that is a thorn in everyone's side.

DRINKING

When I go to Happy Hour, I always order the house vodka in a wine glass with ice, and I ask for tonic on the side, along with a tall glass of water. I've learned that when mixing a drink, I don't need to use high-end vodka. In my case, the tonic blends well with the vodka. You may prefer tomato, cranberry, or pineapple juice with your chosen alcohol. The same rules apply. My theory is that you should reserve high-end vodka or any premium alcohol for when you are drinking it straight. It's crucial to remember that when consuming any alcoholic beverage, you should also drink water. Alcohol dehydrates us, and that can lead to headaches, dizziness, and a horrific hangover. Please remember to order water at the same time you order your drink.

PHARMACEUTICALS

I went to a doctor who told me I had high cholesterol and he wanted to give me a statin drug. I asked, "Can I do it on my own?" He said, "Try." And I did it. I changed my diet and my cholesterol went down. You need medicine, but don't overdose yourself. I'd like to know who has gone to a doctor and the doctor says you don't need a prescription. They are very free to write it.

I had prolapse of the bladder. I was ninety-two when I had the surgery. It was done by a gynecologic oncologist. He said my insides were better than those of a 40-year-old. I believe that is because my body has not been inundated with medicine.

INVESTING

I learned the hard way. I trusted a financial advisor at a major wealth management company and didn't keep a close eye on my account, and by the time I woke up I was down in all my accounts. He never called to advise me to sell something that was on its way down and move the money into something else. I did much better in an account elsewhere that I managed myself.

I always buy the utility of where I reside because it pays a dividend. As well, utility stocks manage to hold their value. We all always need electricity.

If you want to do an option, follow the stock and see if it's going up or down. Weeks could go by and I don't do an option because the return is not good. Only do an option with what you can afford. If the stock is put to you, make sure you have the money to cover it.

TRAVELING

Don't be afraid to travel. Know your limitations. If you need a wheelchair to get around the airport, order one. If you have issues with a leaky bottom, wear pads and/or Depends. But don't let this stop you from going out and doing things.

My daughter once asked if I would like to go on a transatlantic cruise. Let the adventure begin! I had to take an early morning flight from Fort Lauderdale to JFK, which I did alone. I needed to catch an evening flight to the UK to get on the ship the following day. The reason I took the early flight is because airlines are notorious for cancelling flights and I didn't want to lose my connection. I brought my lightweight collapsible wheelchair, which was stored in the cabin. You just need to let the airline know in advance and give them the dimensions. There is limited storage space on the aircraft, so don't wait to do so.

This is a big adventure for someone who is 100.

I always travel with a small empty water bottle and once I go through security, I fill it up because it's much easier for me to pick up a bottle than a paper cup with water.

If your strength in your hands have weakened with age, like mine, the person next to you will be happy to help you. Do you know how many times I have asked the person sitting by me on the plane to open my pretzels, almonds, or other snacks that the flight attendant gave me?

Find a nice person to help you put your bag up in the overhead compartment. Or a flight attendant can help.

To prepare for this adventure, I rented a scooter for the ship and used it at a few ports to get around. I was surprised at how many seniors on the cruise asked me, "How did you get a scooter?" Investigate your options. Know your limitations and compensate for them.

For example, as I mentioned before, I have a leaky bladder, so I make sure I pack enough pads to carry me through the entire vacation, and then some. I won't let this problem prevent me from doing what I want to do.

Cruising

Cruising is a great vacation. You unpack once. And then you visit all the ports.

Medications and Supplements

Make sure you have packed enough for your trip, and then some extra. Always keep your meds and all your valuables in your carry-on bag. I always take a Z-Pak, Covid tests, and Paxlovid just in case I get ill.

Packing

Always keep a small collapsible umbrella in your bag and a lightweight raincoat.

I have a flair for putting myself together. Coordinate your outfits before you pack. I take one bottom and three different tops that will go with it. You have to plan in advance. You will always need a wrap in case it is cool. Then plan all your accessories, including which shoes, purse, and jewelry you will wear with your outfits. If you feel you can't do it, find someone to help you. I always pack clothespins so I can wash my undergarments and socks on a regular basis. If I know I am going away for a long time, I pack clothing that doesn't wrinkle that I can wash by hand and that will dry fast, such as lightweight fabrics.

Documents

Make sure you have both a hard and digital copy of your essential documents such as your passport, driver's license, and medical insurance card, in case you lose them.

Travel Insurance

Most American medical insurance providers will either not cover you or have limited coverage when you are abroad. Take out a travel insurance plan to cover your medical expenses and personal property.

HAVE A PLAN

Work with a physical therapist to set up a plan that teaches you how to get up in different rooms in your home if you should fall. I recently dropped my keys at my front door and accidentally stepped on them, which caused me to fall. I was not worried, as I had a plan in place. I relaxed on the floor for a few minutes to catch my breath, and then I carried out the plan. I scooted on my butt over to my kitchen sink where I have a padded mat on the floor. There I was able to get on my knees, grab the sink, and lift myself up.

I have a strategy for each room of my house. For example, in my bedroom, where I have hard floors, I scoot over on my butt where I can grab a pillow to put on the floor and lean my knees on it as I hold onto the frame of the bed and lift myself up. Learning this has taken the fear out of falling in my house and being stranded alone on the floor.

BATHROOM

When I take a shower, I make sure I have my cell phone and my landline nearby. I place the alert that I wear around my neck on the floor near the door of the shower. You must be prepared in case you fall in the shower and need to contact someone. You should also make sure you have your shower equipped for your needs. I have a handicap bar and teak wood stool I can sit on. Plus, I have two showerheads, one of which is handheld.

A few years ago, I broke my shoulder. Afterwards, I had handicap bars installed on both sides of my toilet, which makes it possible to get up from my toilet by myself.

PROTECTING YOURSELF

If you are living on your own, install surveillance cameras at your entrances. Make sure you pay for the plan where they are recorded and held for a certain period of time. If you hear any noises, you can always go on your app to see if someone is at your door.

No matter how far away she is, my daughter keeps an eye on me. If you are at ease with someone caring for you and keeping a watchful eye, I suggest installing cameras in your home to ensure your safety in case of an accident. Once I fell off my bed and I couldn't get up. My daughter, who was 2000 miles away, noticed this when checking on me through the app. She spoke with me through the camera with a microphone and speaker and got me help. This gives me an additional sense of security besides the alert I wear around my neck.

FOOD

Make sure you know which foods agree with you and which do not. Don't put extra stress on your stomach. With that said, don't be afraid to taste new things and try out new cuisines and restaurants. Always having new experiences gives you something to look forward to.

While on the subject of food, when you're home and you haven't gone marketing recently, look in your cupboards and be creative. For example, one night I had just come home from a trip and I took out of my pantry a can of sweet peas, a can of mushrooms, and minute rice. I boiled the minute rice in some chicken broth, boiled an egg and, within a short time, I had a very filling dinner, combining all the ingredients. And of course, for dessert I treated myself to some ice cream and Cool Whip, which are always staples in my house.

Regarding food preparation and kitchen appliances, there are always ways to make things easier. As we age, some of us may lose the strength in our hands, which can make it difficult to open cans. To compensate for this, I use an electric can opener.

If you have a day and you are feeling good, take the time to cook several meals to portion off and put into the freezer. For example, you can make a meatloaf, bake or broil a large piece of fish, and then prepare some side dishes to freeze. Feeling tired or lazy the next day? You will have an instant meal, just by heating it.

DON'T FRET IT

Embracing a lighthearted perspective in life can make all the difference. For example, if I call customer service or tech support, I often end up in a foreign country where these services have been outsourced. These support workers don't understand what I'm saying and I don't understand what they are saying. Instead of getting upset, I laugh at the absurdity of the situation. It's healthier to laugh at these frustrations than get angry and increase your blood pressure. What I often do is ask to be transferred to America to resolve the communication problem. Not taking everything so seriously avoids unnecessary stress.

PROTECT YOUR CAR

I always keep a plastic bottle of water in my car. Remember, it is no longer drinkable if it sits in the car and heats up. However, if you return to your parked car and you see that some birds have had a convention on the roof and/or trunk of your automobile, you can use that water and the paper towels that you must keep in your car to clean it. If the bird poop sits on the paint too long it will remove some of it. It is an acid. So, always think and be prepared.

ADAPTABILITY

Things don't always go according to plan. My daughter was supposed to come down to visit me in Southern Florida—she was going to drive me up to Orlando for a family party. Well, lo and behold, she broke her foot and had to cancel her flight. I had to adapt my way of thinking about getting up to Orlando on my own at 100 years old. I no longer drive long distances. I'm capable, but why would I put myself in that position to drive three to four hours? My options were a train, but although I was willing to take it, my family was against it. Instead, I had to adapt to the thought of finding and paying for a driver. I did and I'm so grateful, as I had a fantastic time! And my family was relieved, knowing I was being driven.

SEARCH YOUR CLOSETS

Before heading to the stores to buy clothing, carefully go through your closets. You might find a gem, as I did. I discovered a navy top trimmed with brown leather that looks stunning. It was folded in my closet, mistaken for a plain navy T-shirt, until I unearthed it from beneath many other tops. Since I've gotten rid of all my high-heeled shoes, I found a pair of black-and-white flat shoes with rubber soles in my closet, perfect for walking and matching many of my outfits. I also have a collection of Crocs. Living in Florida, a place with frequent rain, I wear them often. I have leopard, blue, white, and black pairs. I was thrilled to find the beige Crocs with a black bow buried in my closet; they're all very stylish and practical.

I recall being invited to a wedding and initially thinking I needed to shop for a new dress. When I went into my closet, I found a magnificent silk chiffon dress with a jacket. It turned out to be a hit. I received many compliments. So, don't forget to go through your closets before splurging on something new, especially if you aim to be economical.

APPLY YOUR CREATIVITY

I happen to be very good at sewing. At 100 years old, I still turn on my sewing machine when I need to fix or add a flair to an item of clothing. Recently, I found a pair of white jeans in my closet and since I'm shrinking in height (not width), they were too long. So, I cut the bottom and added a piece of lace. I ended up with a pair of boutique pants. Think about your skills. If you are not handy with a sewing machine, you can use an iron-on patch to add some pizzazz to your pants. Discover, apply and enrich your life through your unique creative talents.

FORGIVE BEFORE YOU GO

Don't go to your grave with regrets. I am lucky - when I was 99 years old, I realized I was a mean mother to Gayle. She had already forgiven me many years before but I refused to admit I had done anything wrong. As the years crept up on me, I felt it was time for me to say I was sorry. I knew Gayle had forgiven me but I had to forgive myself so I could move on. It was time for me to cleanse my soul. Don't put off saying you are sorry until tomorrow. Tomorrow may never come.

CONCLUSION

I want to thank my fans for encouraging me to sit down at my ripe young age of 100 and write a book. Who would have thought, as a centenarian, I would become a first-time published author?

Who knows, I might have another book in me. You'll have to stay tuned.

I hope this little book, filled with my advice and a peek into my life, brings you joy.

To stay in contact, please follow me and Gayle on social media at @glkirschenbaum. Our favorite is Instagram, where we love to interact with our fans. We are also on TikTok and can be reached at email at: info@gaylekirschenbaum.com.

ANNOTATIONS

1920s

Page 25 Left

I was probably two years old here. I'm all dressed up to go to a party in a satin dress. This must have been shot in a professional studio.

Page 25 Right

Gayle insisted on including this poor-quality photo. I'm not sure it's me, but Gayle says it is. She's the family archivist.

1930s

Page 26 Upper Left

Here I am, dressed up for Hawaiian Night in a bungalow colony we went to in the Catskills.

Page 26 Upper Right

I'm not sure what's happening with my hair in this shot. It might not be my best photo, but it's the only one I have with my Brownie camera.

Page 26 Lower Left

This was taken in the Catskills, as there were no fields of grass in Brooklyn. We went up for vacations, but we couldn't spend the entire summer there like others did, as my mother had to work.

Page 26 Lower Right

I'm not sure whose car this was, but it made for a good prop. I'm wearing braided pigtails with a bow at the bottom of each for a little accent and flair.

Page 27 Upper Left

My hair was wavy enough for me to make banana curls. They were fashionable then, as little Shirley Temple wore them in the 1930s.

Page 27 Upper Right

I enjoyed riding horses in Prospect Park, Brooklyn, as long as they didn't go too fast.

Page 27 Lower Left

Wow, I remember this lavender polka-dot dress. This was taken somewhere in Brooklyn. It's almost like a scene from *A Tree Grows in Brooklyn*.

Page 27 Lower Right

I was the first violinist and first chair at my high school graduation at Girls High. I skipped a grade, known as Rapid Advance (RA) back then, allowing me to graduate early.

Page 28 Upper Left

Captured on New Year's Eve, 1941, when Gerry and I were dating. That's a live gardenia in my hair. Gerry was always impeccably dressed; notice he has a hanky in his pocket.

Page 28 Upper Right

This was taken in my mother's house while Gerry was overseas, serving in the South Pacific during WWII. I was going to a wedding. I had a gift for putting myself together.

1940s and 1950s

Page 28 Lower Left

I'm wearing a beaver coat, something I wouldn't wear today, and a hat which I had made. It was felt with beaver trim. In those days, it wasn't difficult or costly to have a hat made.

Page 28 Lower Right

After the war, Gerry came back thirty pounds heavier. I guess they had plenty of food where he was stationed. He worked in Graves Registration, which was fitting as his family owned a funeral home.

Page 29 Upper Left

Gerry and I were attending a Bar Mitzvah. I just love this dress, with the uneven hem and sweetheart neckline. You could wear it today. If only I still owned it and had the figure for it.

Page 29 Upper Right

I was in Miami Beach at my in-laws' home during the war while Gerry was overseas. I grabbed the hose for a drink of water.

Page 29 Lower Left

On holiday in the Catskills. In those days it was common to wear ankle socks with dresses because you never went without socks.

Page 29 Lower Right

Here I am with my parents in the Catskills on vacation. I'm wearing a plaid sun outfit. My mother was always a classy dresser.

Page 30 Upper Left

Taken during our first cruise, this picture is from the *Franconia* ship of the Cunard Line. Departing and returning from New York Harbor, it sailed to the Caribbean.

Page 30 Upper Right

I'm not exactly sure where this was shot. However, I look cute and very tanned.

Page 30 Lower Left

I bought a secondhand wedding dress and put a pillow underneath to appear pregnant. My husband wore a cutaway coat, a white bathing suit bottom, and a collapsible top hat. We made our entrance dancing to "Get Me to the Church on Time," and ended up winning the costume party on the *Franconia* cruise. The following day, people jokingly started giving me baby gifts.

Page 30 Lower Right

Gerry and I always liked to kibbitz when we posed for photos. This was during one of our trips.

Page 31 Upper Left

I don't like the hat, but I'm wearing a beautiful silk dress for this black-tie function. I added the two clips on the side of the neckline to make it more stylish.

Page 31 Upper Right

At my daughter Gayle's Bat Mitzvah, I dressed in a black Russian broadtail suit that I brought back from Israel. To add some color, I wore a pink silk wide-rim hat and Gerry wore a pink shirt.

Page 31 Lower Left
I'm pretty sure this was taken in Israel while I was calling one of my relatives. I love the dome-style phone enclosure.

Page 31 Lower Right
Gerry and I took a tour of Japan and checked into a hotel in Kyoto. We chose the Japanese-style room over the Western one. This was the bathtub in our room.

1970s

Page 32 Upper Left
Gerry was wearing a tuxedo with velvet trim and a velvet bowtie for the black-tie function we attended. I wore a lavender print dress paired with a bracelet adorned with amethyst stones that complemented the colors in my dress.

Page 32 Upper Right
I always packed mix-and-match clothing when I traveled. I jazzed up this outfit with a necklace of rice pearls.

Page 32 Lower Left
This must have been taken at breakfast in the kitchen at home before Gayle and I got dressed, as she was in a flannel nightgown, and I wore a bathrobe.

Page 32 Lower Right
Gayle shot this photo of me when we were in Russia in the mid-70s during the Cold War, under Brezhnev's regime. What an experience!

Page 33 Upper Left

My hair looks like it was just done. Not a strand was out of place. There must have been plenty of hairspray used.

Page 33 Upper Right

Those were the days when I could tuck in my shirt. I look so nice and thin. Gerry, as usual, was dressed impeccably.

Page 33 Lower Left

Here I am on a boat circling New York with the World Trade Center behind me, which I miss. I have vivid memories of watching the towers go up.

Page 33 Lower Right

Gayle made a sketch from this photograph. It was taken in my kitchen on Long Island. I got a long phone cable so I could take the receiver into another room to speak. I talked on the phone a lot back then.

Page 34 Upper Left

Looks like I'm warming myself up with some wine. Gayle organized a ski weekend through my travel agency, and I went along for the après-ski experience.

Page 34 Upper Right

We celebrated our 50th wedding anniversary at a Long Island restaurant. Gayle recorded a video and captured me saying, "I can't believe I've been married fifty years. I feel like I have a young mind trapped in an old body."

1980s and 1990s

Page 34 Lower Left

Gerry and I were in the casino on a cruise ship. Back then, Gerry loved to play the slot machines and I loved to play dice games like craps.

Page 34 Lower Right

This was from one of our cruises. I like that brown vertical-striped shirt that Gerry was wearing.

Page 35 Upper Left

A fellow was staging photographs with military attire and put the hat and jacket on me.

Page 35 Upper Right

American Airlines held a contest for travel agency owners to win a weekend in Los Angeles, all expenses paid, flying first class. You had to dress up like Marilyn Monroe and I won. We were at JFK, and Gerry and I went right on the plane.

Page 35 Lower Left

I'm holding Gayle's 'dog-ter' and my 'grandog-ter', Chelsea, who later starred in the movie *A Dog's Life: A Dogamentary*, which premiered on HBO.

Page 35 Lower Right

I was climbing Dunn's River Falls in Jamaica. Nothing could hold me back. It was very exhilarating.

Page 36 Upper Left

Up until the end, Gerry always looked great. This was shot at the wedding of one of my granddaughters. It's hard to believe that just a couple of months later Gerry would suffer a massive stroke and pass away.

Page 36 Upper Right

This was at Gayle's birthday party in her home and it looked like I was either the bartender or refilling my glass. I love that top so much that I still wear it.

Page 36 Lower Left

Here I am in New York City, visiting Gayle. This was photographed while I was waiting on the subway platform.

Page 36 Lower Right

Gerry and I went out to visit Gayle and her 'dog-ter', Chelsea, in California. We were walking Chelsea by the Santa Monica coast. It was beautiful. Unlike me, Gerry was always a dog lover.

Page 37 Upper Left

Gayle and I are having dinner in Paris on the left bank in Saint-Germain-des-Prés. The city was packed and bustling, as it was during the 2006 World Cup. France was playing against Italy in the final match.

This was taken during the filming of Gayle's short, funny film, *My Nose*, about my campaign to convince her to get a nose job. This particular moment was captured in the plastic surgeon's office when he used a computer to alter Gayle's nose. My efforts were not successful and she kept her original, imperfect nose.

Page 37 Lower Left

Gayle and I look really good in this photo. I was wearing a two-piece top with a transparent bottom layer and a sweater overlay that revealed part of the layer beneath.

2010s

Page 37 Lower Right

I was enjoying large mussels in a Manhattan restaurant. This dish and a glass of wine had me smiling.

Page 38 Upper Left

At my 90th birthday bash, I had a blast dancing on a bar with my pink boa. The bartender got in trouble for allowing me to do that. He told his boss that there were ten men around me and that if I had fallen, they would have caught me.

Page 38 Upper Right

Photographer Tina Buckman captured images for the press for the release of our film, *Look At Us Now, Mother!* Gayle was wearing vintage Parisian eyeglasses that belonged to my deceased sister-in-law.

Page 38 Lower Left

This was photographed by Madeline Bey. It was a loving moment captured on the rooftop of a building in Manhattan's West Village.

Page 38 Lower Right

Gayle and I were in an ice bar in Norway. They gave us coats to wear on top of our jackets. I was still freezing my butt off. This was when we took a cruise through the magnificent Norwegian fjords.

Page 39 Upper Left

This moment happened during a private screening of *Look At Us Now, Mother!* held at NYU. It marked the first time an audience experienced the film. Flying up to New York, I entrusted Gayle without seeing any previews. The response was incredible—a standing ovation. I was awestruck by Gayle's talent, marveling at how she crafted an extraordinary film by intertwining 8 mm home movies, old photos, and present-day footage.

Page 39 Upper Right

Gayle and I were in a therapy session with Lois Braverman, who was the head of Ackerman Institute for Family Therapy at that time. She asked me to look at Gayle and tell her I didn't mean to hurt her and to ask her forgiveness. It was a poignant moment and captured for our film, *Look At Us Now, Mother!*

Page 39 Lower Left

This was one of many Q&A sessions we did after the screening of our film. This was shot at a cinema in the East Village in New York City. I had never done Q&As before, but they came easily to me as I spoke from my heart.

Page 39 Lower Right
This was at the same first screening at NYU. One of Gayle's friends presented me with gorgeous flowers. I was so surprised and grateful.

2020s

Page 40 Upper Left
I'm at brunch, having my favorite Bloody Mary at a waterside restaurant in Lighthouse Point, Florida. It has a thick slice of crispy bacon inside, and the skewer has tomatoes, shrimp, olives, and pickles. Can you top this?

Page 40 Upper Right
Here I am outside the Roxy Hotel in SoHo, about to go in to see a private movie screening. Through Gayle's membership in the Producers Guild of America, she is invited to many of these events. There was not only a Q&A afterward, but a reception with booze and delicious food.

Page 40 Lower Left
Gayle put together a 100th birthday party for me in Florida at an Italian restaurant. I was overwhelmed by the room decorations, including all the large mounted photos on the walls from my life and an extravagant balloon display. My entire family was there. It was a great time.

Page 40 Lower Right
We had a July 4th shindig at my club and my granddaughter painted my face, as there was a costume contest. I knew I was going to win with that face and I did.

Page 41 Upper Left

Gayle and I were enjoying our time on a cruise. We both looked good in this selfie.

Page 41 Upper Right

During my 100th birthday celebration cruise aboard Oceania's stunning ship, *Vista*, I was invited to host a Q&A session, sharing my secrets to longevity with the passengers. Right after, they pulled open the curtains behind me on the stage and the main chefs and officers presented me with a magnificent birthday cake.

Page 41 Lower Left

I was invited on stage by the singer/songwriter Jax during her performance at the Amway Center in Orlando. The stadium held 20,000 people, and they all sang "Happy Birthday" to me. I was flabbergasted.

Page 41 Lower Right

This was on a cruise when I was 99 years old. I was in the hot tub with a frozen mojito, not seen in the photo. I was surrounded by fellow passengers who were shocked to learn my age. We all had a good time.

Printed in the USA
CPSIA information can be obtained
at www.ICGtesting.com
LVHW011152280724
786604LV00005B/749